The Sorrowful Mysteries

AN ILLUSTRATED ROSARY BOOK FOR KIDS AND THEIR FAMILIES

THE ILLUMINATED ROSARY
Revised Edition

TEXT BY JERRY WINDLEY-DAOUST
ORIGINAL CONCEPT BY MARK DAOUST

For an introduction to praying the rosary with this book, see page 92.

The Canticle of Mary (Magnificat)

My soul proclaims the greatness of the Lord;
my spirit rejoices in God my Savior
for he has looked with favor on his lowly servant.
From this day all generations will call me blessed;
the Almighty has done great things for me
and holy is his name.
He has mercy on those who fear him
in every generation.
He has shown the strength of his arm,
and has scattered the proud in their conceit.
He has cast down the mighty from their thrones,
and has lifted up the lowly.
He has filled the hungry with good things,
and the rich he has sent away empty.
He has come to the help of his servant Israel
for he has remembered his promise of mercy,
the promise he made to our fathers,
to Abraham and his children forever.

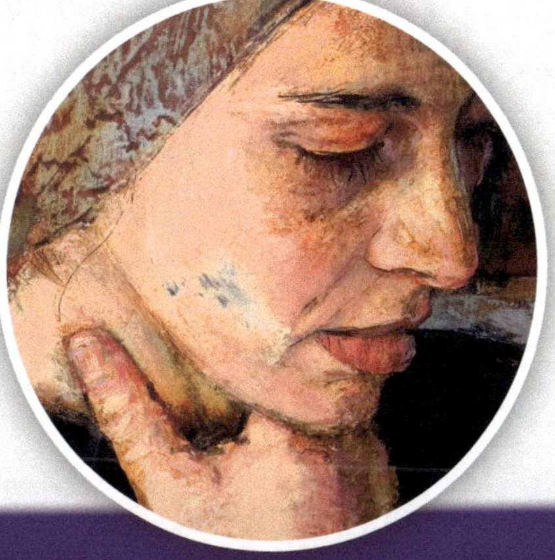

In the name of the Father,
and of the Son, and of the Holy Spirit.
Amen.

I believe
in God, the Father almighty,
Creator of heaven and earth,
and in Jesus Christ,
his only Son, our Lord,
who was conceived by the Holy Spirit,
born of the Virgin Mary,
suffered under Pontius Pilate,
was crucified, died and was buried;
he descended into hell;
on the third day he rose again from the dead;
he ascended into heaven,
and is seated at the right hand
of God the Father almighty;
from there he will come to judge
the living and the dead.

I believe in the Holy Spirit,
the holy catholic Church,
the communion of saints,
the forgiveness of sins,
the resurrection of the body,
and life everlasting.

Amen.

Our Father

who art in heaven,
hallowed be thy name.
Thy kingdom come.
Thy will be done on earth,
as it is in heaven.

Give us this day our daily bread,
and forgive us our trespasses,
as we forgive those
who trespass against us,
and lead us not into temptation,
but deliver us from evil.

Amen.

FOR FAITH

Hail, Mary, full of grace, the Lord is with thee.
Blessed art thou among women,
and blessed is the fruit of thy womb, Jesus.
Holy Mary, Mother of God, pray for us sinners,
now and at the hour of our death. *Amen.*

FOR HOPE

Hail, Mary, full of grace, the Lord is with thee.
Blessed art thou among women,
and blessed is the fruit of thy womb, Jesus.
Holy Mary, Mother of God, pray for us sinners,
now and at the hour of our death. *Amen.*

FOR CHARITY

Hail, Mary, full of grace, the Lord is with thee.
Blessed art thou among women,
and blessed is the fruit of thy womb, Jesus.
Holy Mary, Mother of God, pray for us sinners,
now and at the hour of our death. *Amen.*

Glory be to the Father,
and to the Son, and to the Holy Spirit;
as it was in the beginning, is now, and ever shall be
world without end. *Amen.*

The Agony in the Garden

After Jesus and his disciples
shared the Passover supper,
they went out to a garden to pray.

Jesus said to his disciples,
"My soul is full of sorrow;
stay and keep awake with me."

Then he went a little ways,
threw himself to the ground,
and prayed: "Abba, Father,
if you are willing,
take this cup of suffering
away from me; yet let it be
not as I want,
but what you want."

INTENTIONS

The Agony in the Garden

Our Father
who art in heaven,
hallowed be thy name.
Thy kingdom come.
Thy will be done on earth,
as it is in heaven.

Give us this day our daily bread,
and forgive us our trespasses,
as we forgive those
who trespass against us,
and lead us not into temptation,
but deliver us from evil.

Amen.

The Agony in the Garden

Hail, Mary, full of grace, the Lord is with thee.
Blessed art thou among women,
and blessed is the fruit of thy womb, Jesus.

Holy Mary, Mother of God, pray for us sinners,
now and at the hour of our death. *Amen.*

Hail, Mary, full of grace, the Lord is with thee.
Blessed art thou among women,
and blessed is the fruit of thy womb, Jesus.

Holy Mary, Mother of God, pray for us sinners,
now and at the hour of our death. *Amen.*

The Agony in the Garden

Hail, Mary, full of grace, the Lord is with thee.
Blessed art thou among women,
and blessed is the fruit of thy womb, Jesus.

Holy Mary, Mother of God, pray for us sinners,
now and at the hour of our death. *Amen.*

Hail, Mary, full of grace, the Lord is with thee.
Blessed art thou among women,
and blessed is the fruit of thy womb, Jesus.

Holy Mary, Mother of God, pray for us sinners,
now and at the hour of our death. *Amen.*

The Agony in the Garden

Hail, Mary, full of grace, the Lord is with thee.
Blessed art thou among women,
and blessed is the fruit of thy womb, Jesus.

Holy Mary, Mother of God, pray for us sinners,
now and at the hour of our death. *Amen.*

Hail, Mary, full of grace, the Lord is with thee.
Blessed art thou among women,
and blessed is the fruit of thy womb, Jesus.

Holy Mary, Mother of God, pray for us sinners,
now and at the hour of our death. *Amen.*

The Agony in the Garden

Hail, Mary, full of grace, the Lord is with thee.
Blessed art thou among women,
and blessed is the fruit of thy womb, Jesus.

Holy Mary, Mother of God, pray for us sinners,
now and at the hour of our death. *Amen.*

Hail, Mary, full of grace, the Lord is with thee.
Blessed art thou among women,
and blessed is the fruit of thy womb, Jesus.

Holy Mary, Mother of God, pray for us sinners,
now and at the hour of our death. *Amen.*

The Agony in the Garden

Hail, Mary, full of grace, the Lord is with thee.
Blessed art thou among women,
and blessed is the fruit of thy womb, Jesus.

Holy Mary, Mother of God, pray for us sinners,
now and at the hour of our death. *Amen.*

Hail, Mary, full of grace, the Lord is with thee.
Blessed art thou among women,
and blessed is the fruit of thy womb, Jesus.

Holy Mary, Mother of God, pray for us sinners,
now and at the hour of our death. *Amen.*

The Agony in the Garden

Glory be to the Father,
and to the Son, and to the Holy Spirit;
as it was in the beginning, is now,
and ever shall be, world without end.
Amen.

O my Jesus, forgive us our sins,
save us from the fires of hell;
lead all souls to heaven, especially
those in most need of thy mercy.

The Scourging at the Pillar

Men came and arrested Jesus,
and all his disciples ran away.

The men took Jesus to Pilate,
saying, "This man says
he is the Messiah, a king."

Pilate questioned Jesus:
"Are you the king of the Jews?"

Jesus replied, "You say so."

Pilate said to the people,
"This man has done nothing
to deserve death;
I will have him flogged,
then release him."

INTENTIONS

The Scourging at the Pillar

Our Father

who art in heaven,
hallowed be thy name.
Thy kingdom come.
Thy will be done on earth,
as it is in heaven.

Give us this day our daily bread,
and forgive us our trespasses,
as we forgive those
who trespass against us,
and lead us not into temptation,
but deliver us from evil.

Amen.

The Scourging at the Pillar

Hail, Mary, full of grace, the Lord is with thee.
Blessed art thou among women,
and blessed is the fruit of thy womb, Jesus.

Holy Mary, Mother of God, pray for us sinners,
now and at the hour of our death. *Amen.*

Hail, Mary, full of grace, the Lord is with thee.
Blessed art thou among women,
and blessed is the fruit of thy womb, Jesus.

Holy Mary, Mother of God, pray for us sinners,
now and at the hour of our death. *Amen.*

The Scourging at the Pillar

Hail, Mary, full of grace, the Lord is with thee.
Blessed art thou among women,
and blessed is the fruit of thy womb, Jesus.

Holy Mary, Mother of God, pray for us sinners,
now and at the hour of our death. *Amen.*

Hail, Mary, full of grace, the Lord is with thee.
Blessed art thou among women,
and blessed is the fruit of thy womb, Jesus.

Holy Mary, Mother of God, pray for us sinners,
now and at the hour of our death. *Amen.*

The Scourging at the Pillar

Hail, Mary, full of grace, the Lord is with thee.
Blessed art thou among women,
and blessed is the fruit of thy womb, Jesus.

Holy Mary, Mother of God, pray for us sinners,
now and at the hour of our death. *Amen.*

Hail, Mary, full of grace, the Lord is with thee.
Blessed art thou among women,
and blessed is the fruit of thy womb, Jesus.

Holy Mary, Mother of God, pray for us sinners,
now and at the hour of our death. *Amen.*

The Scourging at the Pillar

Hail, Mary, full of grace, the Lord is with thee.
Blessed art thou among women,
and blessed is the fruit of thy womb, Jesus.

Holy Mary, Mother of God, pray for us sinners,
now and at the hour of our death. *Amen.*

Hail, Mary, full of grace, the Lord is with thee.
Blessed art thou among women,
and blessed is the fruit of thy womb, Jesus.

Holy Mary, Mother of God, pray for us sinners,
now and at the hour of our death. *Amen.*

The Scourging at the Pillar

Hail, Mary, full of grace, the Lord is with thee.
Blessed art thou among women,
and blessed is the fruit of thy womb, Jesus.

Holy Mary, Mother of God, pray for us sinners,
now and at the hour of our death. *Amen.*

Hail, Mary, full of grace, the Lord is with thee.
Blessed art thou among women,
and blessed is the fruit of thy womb, Jesus.

Holy Mary, Mother of God, pray for us sinners,
now and at the hour of our death. *Amen.*

The Scourging at the Pillar

Glory be to the Father,
and to the Son, and to the Holy Spirit;
as it was in the beginning, is now,
and ever shall be, world without end.
Amen.

O my Jesus, forgive us our sins,
save us from the fires of hell;
lead all souls to heaven, especially
those in most need of thy mercy.

The Crowning with Thorns

The soldiers clothed Jesus
in a purple cloak, and placed
a crown of thorns on his head.

They made fun of him, saying,
"Hail, King of the Jews!"
They spat on him and hit his face,
and struck his head with a reed.

Then Pilate showed Jesus to the people.
"Here is the man!" Pilate said.
"Here is your king!"

But the people shouted,
"Away with him! Crucify him!"

So Pilate did as the people asked,
and handed him over to be crucified.

INTENTIONS

The Crowning with Thorns

Our Father
who art in heaven,
hallowed be thy name.
Thy kingdom come.
Thy will be done on earth,
as it is in heaven.

Give us this day our daily bread,
and forgive us our trespasses,
as we forgive those
who trespass against us,
and lead us not into temptation,
but deliver us from evil.

Amen.

The Crowning with Thorns

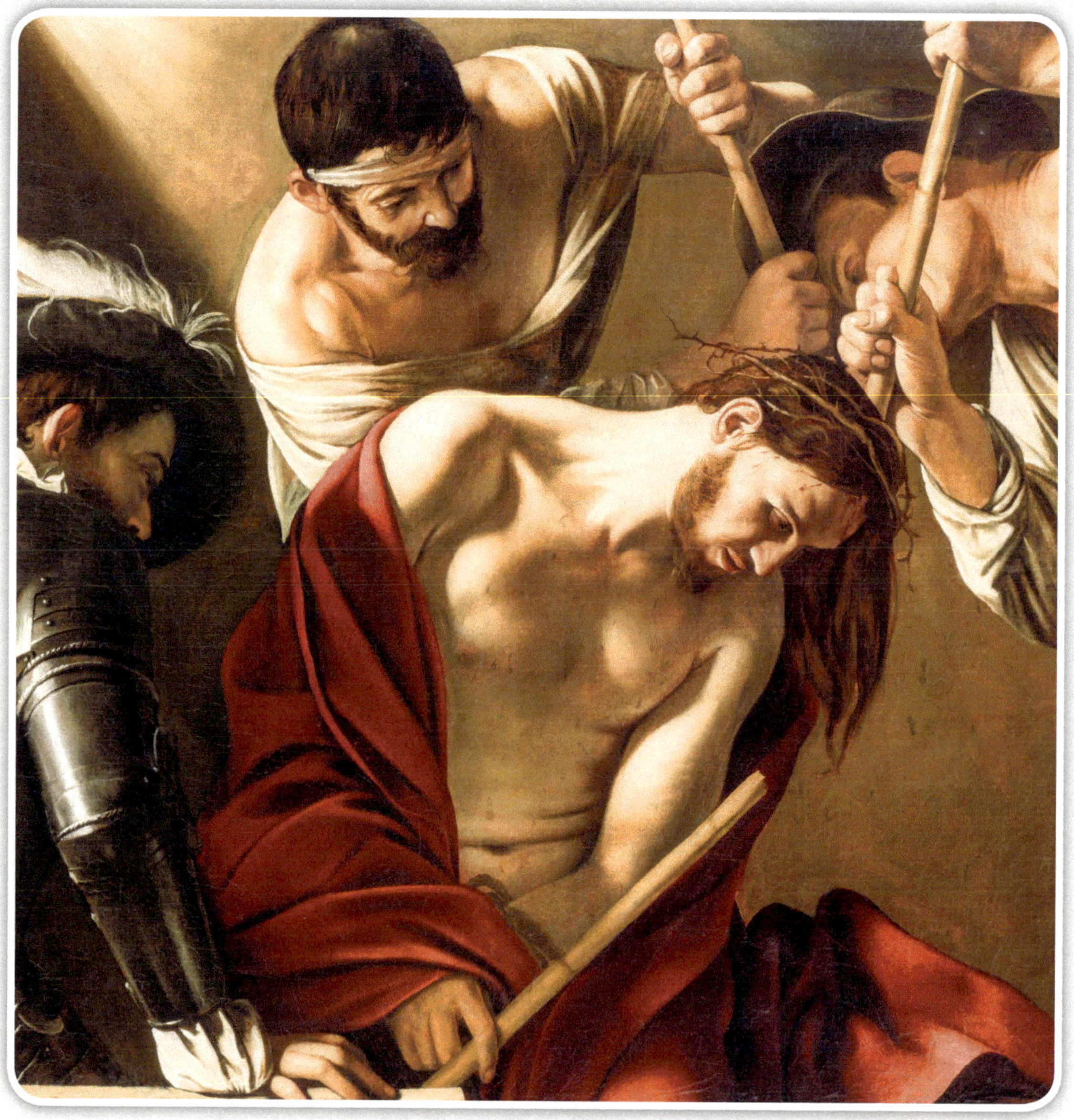

Hail, Mary, full of grace, the Lord is with thee.
Blessed art thou among women,
and blessed is the fruit of thy womb, Jesus.

Holy Mary, Mother of God, pray for us sinners,
now and at the hour of our death. *Amen.*

Hail, Mary, full of grace, the Lord is with thee.
Blessed art thou among women,
and blessed is the fruit of thy womb, Jesus.

Holy Mary, Mother of God, pray for us sinners,
now and at the hour of our death. *Amen.*

The Crowning with Thorns

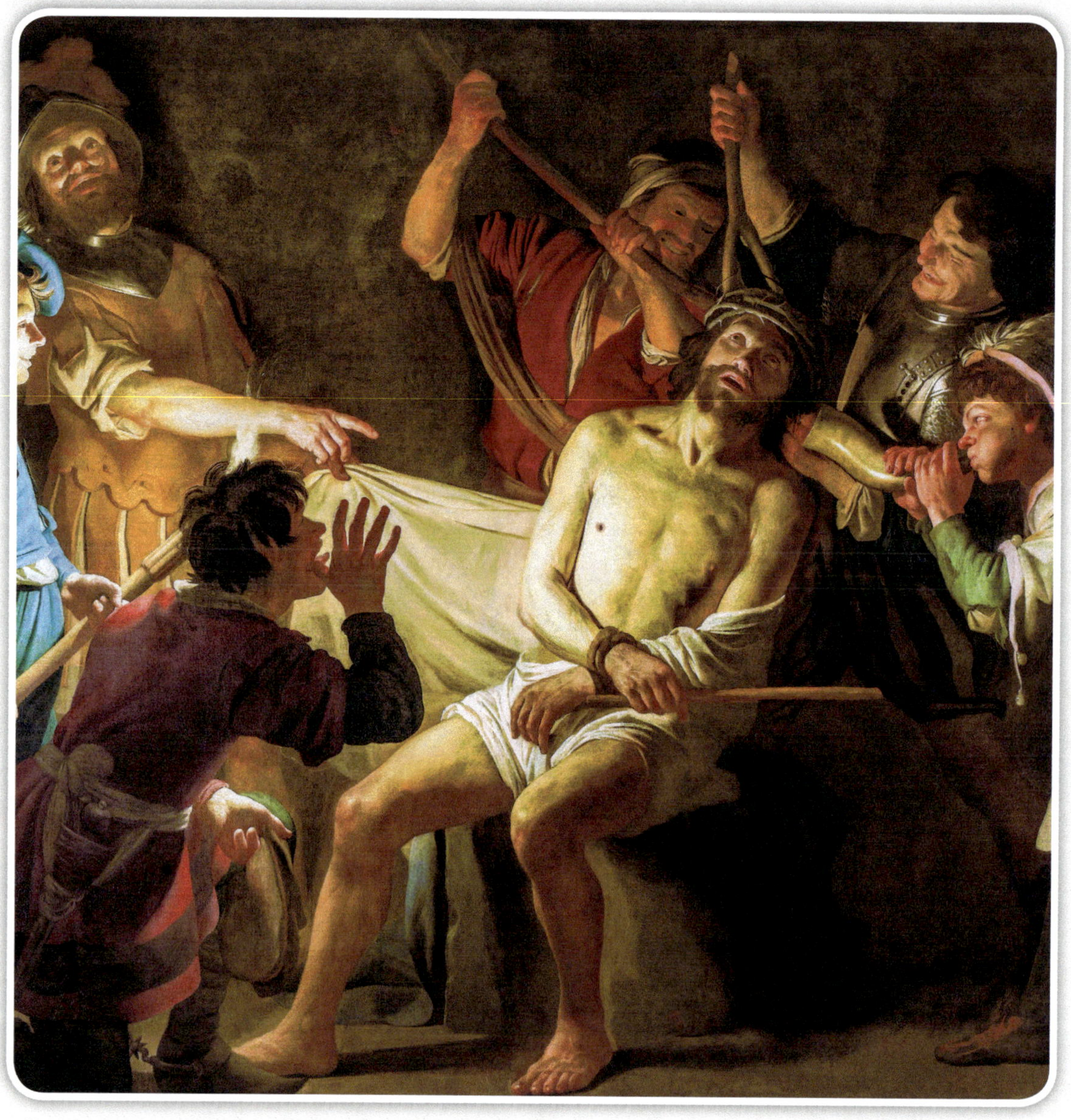

Hail, Mary, full of grace, the Lord is with thee.
Blessed art thou among women,
and blessed is the fruit of thy womb, Jesus.

Holy Mary, Mother of God, pray for us sinners,
now and at the hour of our death. *Amen.*

Hail, Mary, full of grace, the Lord is with thee.
Blessed art thou among women,
and blessed is the fruit of thy womb, Jesus.

Holy Mary, Mother of God, pray for us sinners,
now and at the hour of our death. *Amen.*

The Crowning with Thorns

Hail, Mary, full of grace, the Lord is with thee.
Blessed art thou among women,
and blessed is the fruit of thy womb, Jesus.

Holy Mary, Mother of God, pray for us sinners,
now and at the hour of our death. *Amen.*

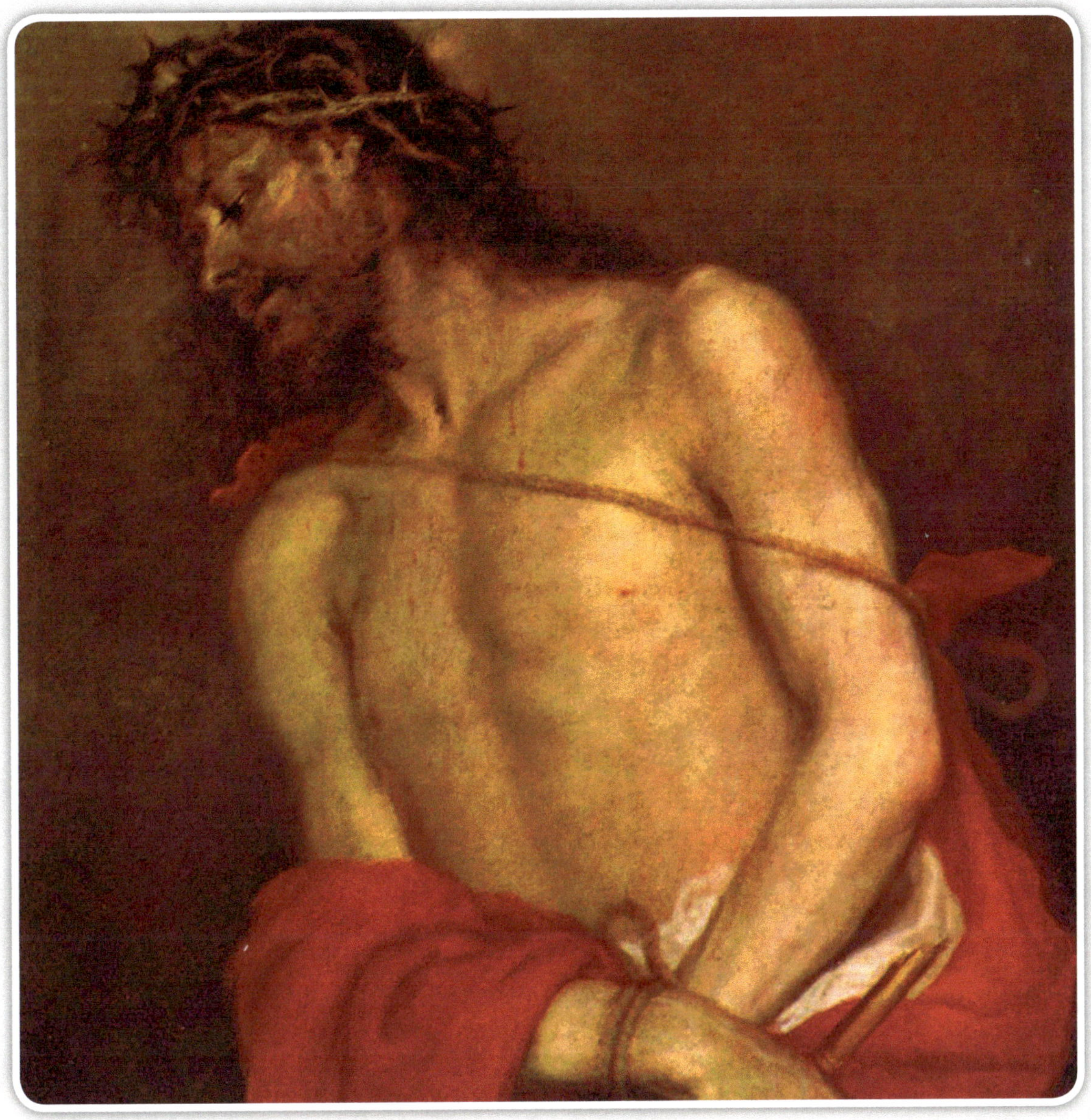

Hail, Mary, full of grace, the Lord is with thee.
Blessed art thou among women,
and blessed is the fruit of thy womb, Jesus.

Holy Mary, Mother of God, pray for us sinners,
now and at the hour of our death. *Amen.*

The Crowning with Thorns

Hail, Mary, full of grace, the Lord is with thee.
Blessed art thou among women,
and blessed is the fruit of thy womb, Jesus.

Holy Mary, Mother of God, pray for us sinners,
now and at the hour of our death. *Amen.*

Hail, Mary, full of grace, the Lord is with thee.
Blessed art thou among women,
and blessed is the fruit of thy womb, Jesus.

Holy Mary, Mother of God, pray for us sinners,
now and at the hour of our death. *Amen.*

The Crowning with Thorns

Hail, Mary, full of grace, the Lord is with thee.
Blessed art thou among women,
and blessed is the fruit of thy womb, Jesus.

Holy Mary, Mother of God, pray for us sinners,
now and at the hour of our death. *Amen.*

Hail, Mary, full of grace, the Lord is with thee.
Blessed art thou among women,
and blessed is the fruit of thy womb, Jesus.

Holy Mary, Mother of God, pray for us sinners,
now and at the hour of our death. *Amen.*

The Crowning with Thorns

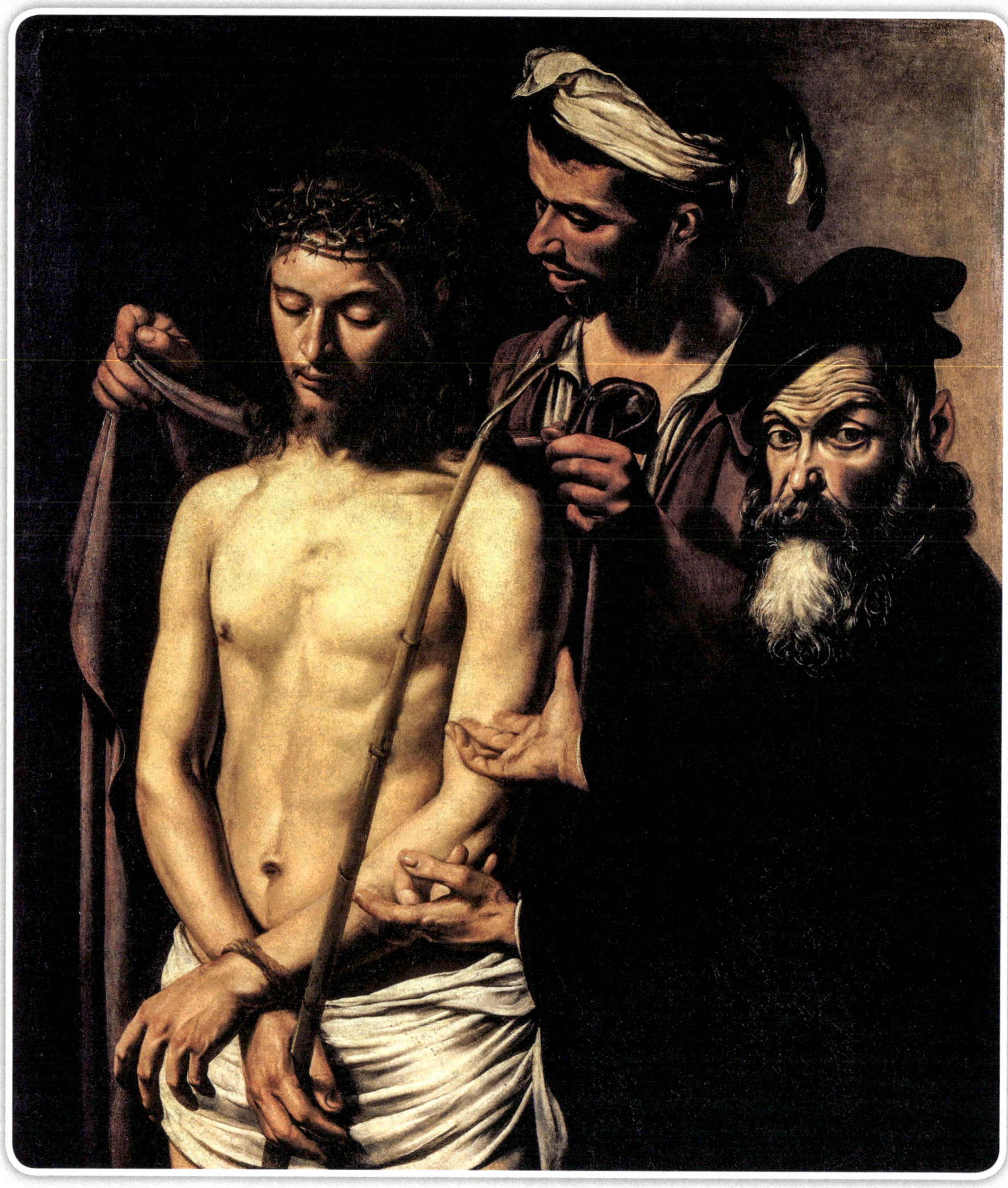

Glory be to the Father,
and to the Son, and to the Holy Spirit;
as it was in the beginning, is now,
and ever shall be, world without end.
Amen.

O my Jesus, forgive us our sins,
save us from the fires of hell;
lead all souls to heaven, especially
those in most need of thy mercy.

The Carrying of the Cross

As they led Jesus out to crucify him,
they seized a man, Simon of Cyrene,
and laid the cross on him,
making him carry it behind Jesus.

And his friends remembered
what Jesus had told them:
"If any want to become my followers,
let them deny themselves
and take up their cross and follow me.
For those who want to save their life
will lose it,
and those who lose their life
for my sake, and for the sake of the gospel,
will save it."

INTENTIONS

The Carrying of the Cross

Our Father
who art in heaven,
hallowed be thy name.
Thy kingdom come.
Thy will be done on earth,
as it is in heaven.

Give us this day our daily bread,
and forgive us our trespasses,
as we forgive those
who trespass against us,
and lead us not into temptation,
but deliver us from evil.

Amen.

The Carrying of the Cross

Hail, Mary, full of grace, the Lord is with thee.
Blessed art thou among women,
and blessed is the fruit of thy womb, Jesus.

Holy Mary, Mother of God, pray for us sinners,
now and at the hour of our death. *Amen.*

Hail, Mary, full of grace, the Lord is with thee.
Blessed art thou among women,
and blessed is the fruit of thy womb, Jesus.

Holy Mary, Mother of God, pray for us sinners,
now and at the hour of our death. *Amen.*

The Carrying of the Cross

Hail, Mary, full of grace, the Lord is with thee.
Blessed art thou among women,
and blessed is the fruit of thy womb, Jesus.

Holy Mary, Mother of God, pray for us sinners,
now and at the hour of our death. *Amen.*

Hail, Mary, full of grace, the Lord is with thee.
Blessed art thou among women,
and blessed is the fruit of thy womb, Jesus.

Holy Mary, Mother of God, pray for us sinners,
now and at the hour of our death. *Amen.*

The Carrying of the Cross

Hail, Mary, full of grace, the Lord is with thee.
Blessed art thou among women,
and blessed is the fruit of thy womb, Jesus.

Holy Mary, Mother of God, pray for us sinners,
now and at the hour of our death. *Amen.*

Hail, Mary, full of grace, the Lord is with thee.
Blessed art thou among women,
and blessed is the fruit of thy womb, Jesus.

Holy Mary, Mother of God, pray for us sinners,
now and at the hour of our death. *Amen.*

The Carrying of the Cross

Hail, Mary, full of grace, the Lord is with thee.
Blessed art thou among women,
and blessed is the fruit of thy womb, Jesus.

Holy Mary, Mother of God, pray for us sinners,
now and at the hour of our death. *Amen.*

Hail, Mary, full of grace, the Lord is with thee.
Blessed art thou among women,
and blessed is the fruit of thy womb, Jesus.

Holy Mary, Mother of God, pray for us sinners,
now and at the hour of our death. *Amen.*

The Carrying of the Cross

Hail, Mary, full of grace, the Lord is with thee.
Blessed art thou among women,
and blessed is the fruit of thy womb, Jesus.

Holy Mary, Mother of God, pray for us sinners,
now and at the hour of our death. *Amen.*

Hail, Mary, full of grace, the Lord is with thee.
Blessed art thou among women,
and blessed is the fruit of thy womb, Jesus.

Holy Mary, Mother of God, pray for us sinners,
now and at the hour of our death. *Amen.*

The Carrying of the Cross

Glory be to the Father,
and to the Son, and to the Holy Spirit;
as it was in the beginning, is now,
and ever shall be, world without end.
Amen.

O my Jesus, forgive us our sins,
save us from the fires of hell;
lead all souls to heaven, especially
those in most need of thy mercy.

The Crucifixion

They crucified him and two criminals
at a place called The Skull.

"Father, forgive them," Jesus said,
"for they do not know what they are doing."
And his disciples remembered
the words of the Prophet Isaiah:

He was a man of suffering, knowing pain;
yet it was our pain that he bore,
and our sufferings that he endured.
He was pierced for our sins,
crushed for our iniquity.
He bore the punishment that makes us whole;
by his wounds we were healed.

In the afternoon, as the sun's light failed,
Jesus cried out, "Father, into your hands
I commend my spirit."
And he breathed his last.

INTENTIONS

ESVS NAZA
RENVS REX

The Crucifixion

Our Father
who art in heaven,
hallowed be thy name.
Thy kingdom come.
Thy will be done on earth,
as it is in heaven.

Give us this day our daily bread,
and forgive us our trespasses,
as we forgive those
who trespass against us,
and lead us not into temptation,
but deliver us from evil.

Amen.

INRI

The Crucifixion

Hail, Mary, full of grace, the Lord is with thee.
Blessed art thou among women,
and blessed is the fruit of thy womb, Jesus.

Holy Mary, Mother of God, pray for us sinners,
now and at the hour of our death. *Amen.*

Hail, Mary, full of grace, the Lord is with thee.
Blessed art thou among women,
and blessed is the fruit of thy womb, Jesus.

Holy Mary, Mother of God, pray for us sinners,
now and at the hour of our death. *Amen.*

The Crucifixion

Hail, Mary, full of grace, the Lord is with thee.
Blessed art thou among women,
and blessed is the fruit of thy womb, Jesus.

Holy Mary, Mother of God, pray for us sinners,
now and at the hour of our death. *Amen.*

Hail, Mary, full of grace, the Lord is with thee.
Blessed art thou among women,
and blessed is the fruit of thy womb, Jesus.

Holy Mary, Mother of God, pray for us sinners,
now and at the hour of our death. *Amen.*

The Crucifixion

Hail, Mary, full of grace, the Lord is with thee.
Blessed art thou among women,
and blessed is the fruit of thy womb, Jesus.

Holy Mary, Mother of God, pray for us sinners,
now and at the hour of our death. *Amen.*

Hail, Mary, full of grace, the Lord is with thee.
Blessed art thou among women,
and blessed is the fruit of thy womb, Jesus.

Holy Mary, Mother of God, pray for us sinners,
now and at the hour of our death. *Amen.*

The Crucifixion

Hail, Mary, full of grace, the Lord is with thee.
Blessed art thou among women,
and blessed is the fruit of thy womb, Jesus.

Holy Mary, Mother of God, pray for us sinners,
now and at the hour of our death. *Amen.*

Hail, Mary, full of grace, the Lord is with thee.
Blessed art thou among women,
and blessed is the fruit of thy womb, Jesus.

Holy Mary, Mother of God, pray for us sinners,
now and at the hour of our death. *Amen.*

The Crucifixion

Hail, Mary, full of grace, the Lord is with thee.
Blessed art thou among women,
and blessed is the fruit of thy womb, Jesus.

Holy Mary, Mother of God, pray for us sinners,
now and at the hour of our death. *Amen.*

Hail, Mary, full of grace, the Lord is with thee.
Blessed art thou among women,
and blessed is the fruit of thy womb, Jesus.

Holy Mary, Mother of God, pray for us sinners,
now and at the hour of our death. *Amen.*

The Crucifixion

Glory be to the Father,
and to the Son, and to the Holy Spirit;
as it was in the beginning, is now,
and ever shall be, world without end.
Amen.

O my Jesus, forgive us our sins,
save us from the fires of hell;
lead all souls to heaven, especially
those in most need of thy mercy.

Hail, holy Queen,
Mother of Mercy:
our life, our sweetness and our hope.
To thee do we cry,
poor banished children of Eve;
To thee do we send up our sighs,
mourning and weeping in this valley of tears.
Turn then, most gracious advocate,
thine eyes of mercy toward us;
and after this our exile,
show unto us the blessed fruit of thy womb, Jesus.
O clement, O loving,
O sweet Virgin Mary.

V. Pray for us, O holy Mother of God.

R. That we may be made worthy of the
promises of Christ.

In the name of the Father, and of the Son,
and of the Holy Spirit. *Amen.*

Art Credits

All works are in the public domain, except as otherwise noted.

Cover: Diego Velázquez, *Christ Crucified*, 1632.

Title page, 23, 39, 55, 71, 87, back cover: Jessica Connelly, *Sorrowful Mysteries Rose Wreath*, 2018. Artist website: telosartshop.com

Title Page: Diego Velazquez, *Christ Crucified*, 1632.

2–3: Bruce Herman, *Called* (from the series Woman), 2006. Used with permission. Artist website: bruceherman.com.

5: A.N. Mironov, *He Is Risen*, 2008. Licensed under CC BY-SA 4.0. Artist website: artmiro.ru

7: Simon Bening, *The Seven Sorrows of the Virgin*, 1525–1530.

The Agony in the Garden

8–9: Goddard & Gibbs, *Agony in the Garden of Gesthemane*, 1973. Immaculate Heart of Mary (Hayes, Middlesex, UK). Photo by G. Licence.

10–11: Lucas Cranach the Elder, *The Garden of Gethsemane*, 1518. National Museum of Western Art (Tokyo).

12: George Richmond, *The Agony in the Garden*, 1858.

13: Carle Vanloo, *The Agony in the Garden*, 1760.

14: Andrea Mantegna, Altarpiece of San Zeno in Verona, 1459.

15: Giorgio Vasari, *The Garden of Gethsemane*, 1570.

16: Eugène Delacroix, *The Agony in the Garden*, 1851.

17: Martin Johann Schmidt, *Christ on the Mount of Olives*, 18th century.

18: Giulio Cesare Procaccini, *The Agony in the Garden*, 1616–1620.

19: Josef August Untersberger, *Christ on the Mount of Olives*, c. 1920s.

20: El Greco, *The Agony in the Garden of Gethsemane*, c. 1590.

21: Bernard van Orley, *Four Scenes from the Passion*, c. 1520.

22: Caravaggio, *The Taking of Christ*, 1602.

The Scourging at the Pillar

24–25: Josè De Madrazo y Agudo, *Jesus in the House of Annas*, 1803.

26–27: Gerard van Honthorst, *Christ Before the High Priest*, 1617.

28–29: Vasily Polenov, *He is Guilty of Death*, 1906.

30–31: Caravaggio, *Christ at the Column*, 1607.

32: Luca di Tommè, *The Flagellation*, 1365.

33: Unknown Artist, *The Scourging*, 1503–1504.

34: James Tissot, *The Scourging on the Back*, 1886–1894. Image provided by Felix Just, S.J.

35: William-Adolphe Bouguereau, *The Flagellation of Christ*, 1880.

36: Bruce Herman, *The Flogging* (from the series Golgotha), 1991. All rights reserved. Used with permission. Artist website: bruceherman.com

37: Anton Raphael Mengs, *The Flagellation of Christ*, 1769.

38: Lehman & Bolton, *Christ Falls Exhausted after the Scourging*, 1888.

The Crowning with Thorns

40–41: Matthias Stom, *Christ Crowned with Thorns*, 1633–1639.

42–43: Jan Miense Molenaer, *Christ Mocked and Crowned with Thorns*, 1639.

44: Caravaggio, *The Crowning with Thorns*, 1602–1604.

45: Gerard van Honthorst, *The Mocking of Christ*, 1617.

46: Gerard van Honthorst, *Christ Crowned with Thorns*, 1622.

47: Édouard Manet, *Jesus Mocked by the Soldiers*, 1864–1865.

48: A. Carracci, *Jesus Is Exhibited to the People Wearing a Crown of Thorns*, 1587. Licensed under CC BY-SA 4.0. Image courtesy Wellcome Collection.

49: Mateo Cerezo, *Ecce Homo*, 1650.

50: Hendrick ter Brugghen, *Christ Crowned with Thorns*, 1620.

51: Correggio, *Head of Christ*, 1525–1530.

52: Antonio Ciseri, *Ecce Homo*, 1862.

53: Mihály Munkácsy, *Ecce Homo*, 1896.

54: Caravaggio, *Ecce Homo*, 1605.

The Carrying of the Cross

56–57: Anthony Van Dyck, *The Carrying of the Cross*, c. 1630s. Licensed from Adobe Stock.

58–59: Unknown, *Christ Bearing the Cross*, 15th century.

60: Matthew James Collins, *Jesus Carrying the Cross*, 2010. All rights reserved. Used with permission. Artist website: matthewjamescollins.com

61: Titian, *Christ Carrying the Cross*, 1565.

62: Yann Forget, *Jesus Falls the First Time*, 2009. © Yann Forget / Wikimedia Commons / CC–BY-SA–3.0.

63: James Tissot, *Jesus Meets His Mother*, 1886–1894.

64: Unknown, *Christ Falls on the Road to Calvary*, 1570s.

65: Raphael, *Christ Falling on the Way to Calvary*, 1516.

66: Unknown, from the Stations of the Cross in the church of Maria am Gestade, c. 19th century. Licensed from Adobe Stock.

67: Unknown, from the Stations of the Cross in the church of Maria am Gestade, c. 19th century. Licensed from Adobe Stock.

68: El Greco, *Christ Carrying the Cross*, 1577–1587.

69: C. A. Wauters, from the Stations of the Cross in the church of Notre Dame du Finstere, 19th century. Licensed from Adobe Stock.

70: Anthony Van Dyck, *Christ Carrying the Cross*, early 17th century.

The Crucifixion

72–73: Peter Paul Rubens, *The Elevation of the Cross by Rubens*, 1610–1611.

74–75: Bardi Barth, Mysteries of the Rosary: *Tree of Life*. Copyright © HERBRONNEN vzw; all rights reserved. Used with permission. Artist website: www.bradi-barth.org

76: Master of the Fiesole Epiphany, *Christ on the Cross with Saints Vincent Ferrer, John the Baptist, Mark and Antoninus*, 1491/1495.

77: Andreas Pavias, *The Crucifixion*, 15th century.

78: Albrecht Dürer, *Adoration of the Trinity*, 1511.

79: James Tissot, *It Is Finished (Consummatum Est)*, 1886–1894.

80: Pedro Orrente, *The Crucifixion*, 1625–1630.

81: John Martin, *Calvary*, 1830–1840.

82: Diego Velázquez, *Christ Crucified*, 1632.

83: Daniel Bonnell, *Eucharist*, 2009. All rights reserved. Used with permission. Artist website: bonnellart.com

84: Giovanni Benedetto Castiglione, *Crucifixion*, c.1660.

85: Peter Paul Rubens, *Descent from the Cross*, 1612–1614. Photography by Joaquim Alves Gaspar. Licensed under CC BY-SA 4.0.

86: Peter Paul Rubens, *The Entombment*, 1612.

88: William Adolphe Bouguereau, *Pietà*, 1876.

Back cover: El Greco, *Christ Carrying the Cross*, 1577–1587.

How to Pray the Rosary with This Book

WELCOME to The Illuminated Rosary, a way of praying the rosary more meditatively with the help of sacred art. The Illuminated Rosary was first developed for families with young children, but has proven popular with young and old alike.

Using The Illuminated Rosary is simple:

- The *full text* of every prayer is printed in order, so that young readers might learn to pray the rosary without distraction.
- Each mystery is introduced with a brief, *child-friendly reading* loosely based on the Scriptures. In the rosary, a mystery is an episode in the life of Christ or Mary that unfolds God's plan of salvation. After reading about each mystery, you will be prompted to state the *intentions* for which you are praying.
- The *sacred art* on every spread is meant to aid prayerful meditation. As you pray each decade, remember the words of Pope Paul VI: "By its nature the recitation of the Rosary calls for a quiet rhythm and a lingering pace, helping the individual to meditate on the mysteries of the Lord's life..." (Pope Paul VI, Marialis Cultus #47).
- The roses around the text of each Hail Mary serve as *rosary beads*, helping kids keep track of where they are in the decade.

Here are some practical suggestions for praying The Illuminated Rosary with children:

- *Keep it short* at first, saying one decade of the rosary in a single sitting. *Try praying antiphonally*: one group or person says the first half of each prayer, and the other group or person says the second half.
- Optionally, *ask your family for intentions* for each decade. For whom or for what do you wish to offer the prayers of the decade?
- After you are finished praying, *ask your children what thoughts or feelings* they had as they meditated on each mystery. Which artwork "spoke" to them most? How might the Holy Spirit have been speaking to them through their meditation?

You may find some of the artwork in these pages not to your personal taste. That is natural; but to get the most out of your meditation, try viewing these images sympathetically. Let the vision of the artist challenge you: Why would the artist paint the mystery as he or she did? What does it reveal to the artist and others who have appreciated it? However you use The Illuminated Rosary, may praying with it lead you closer to the heart of Jesus through the heart of his mother; and may your own heart be filled with awe, reverence, and wonder.

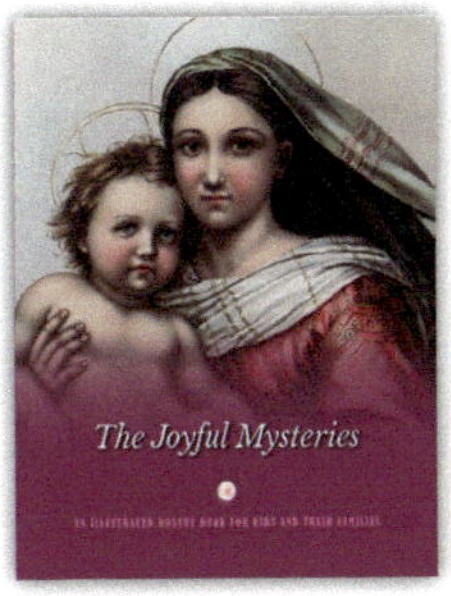

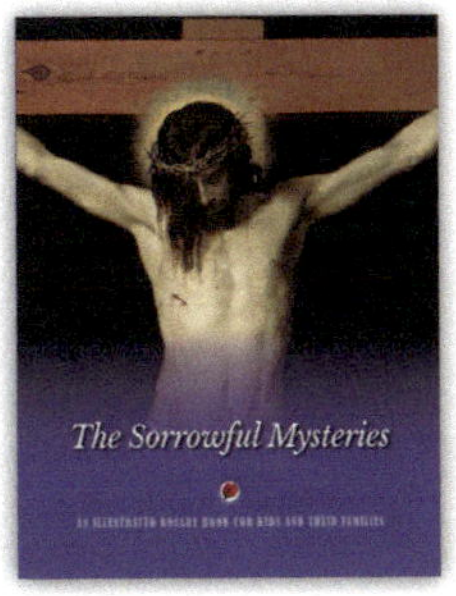

Dedicated to the memory of Norman G. Daoust.

Nihil obstat:
Rev. Timothy Hall, *Censor librorum*

Imprimatur:
†Most Rev. John M. Quinn, Bishop of Winona
February 12, 2015

The imprimatur is an official declaration that a book or pamphlet is free of doctrinal or moral error. No implication is contained therein that those who have granted the imprimatur agree with the contents, opinions, or statements expressed.

The Illuminated Rosary, Revised Edition
The Sorrowful Mysteries
An Illustrated Rosary Book for Kids and Their Families

29 28 27 26 25 5 6 7 8 9 10

ISBN: 978-1-68192-512-7 (Inventory No. T2401)
JUVENILE NONFICTION / Religion / Devotional & Prayer
JUVENILE NONFICTION / Religion / Christianity / Christian Life
RELIGION / Christianity / Catholic
LCCN: 2019939986

Book design and build by Steve Nagel.
Acknowledgments assistance by Sara Dethloff.
Proofingb y Karen Carter.

See art credits, page 90, for copyright statements pertaining to individual artworks.

Our Sunday Visitor Publishing
www.osv.com